THE
LITTLE BOOK OF
SELF-CARE
FOR
VIRGO

*Simple Ways to Refresh
and Restore—According
to the Stars*

CONSTANCE STELLAS

ADAMS M[...]

NEW YORK LONDON TORONTO

T0019302

Adamsmedia

Adams Media
An Imprint of Simon & Schuster, Inc.
100 Technology Center Drive
Stoughton, MA 02072

First Adams Media hardcover edition January 2019

ADAMS MEDIA and colophon are trademarks of Simon & Schuster.

For information about special discounts for bulk purchases,
please contact Simon & Schuster Special Sales at 1-866-506-1949
or business@simonandschuster.com.

The Simon & Schuster Speakers Bureau can bring authors to your live event. For
more information or to book an event contact the Simon & Schuster Speakers
Bureau at 1-866-248-3049 or visit our website at www.simonspeakers.com.

Interior design by Colleen Cunningham
Interior images © Getty Images; Clipart.com

Manufactured in China

10 9

Library of Congress Cataloging-in-Publication Data has been applied for.

ISBN 978-1-5072-0974-5
ISBN 978-1-5072-0975-2 (ebook)

Dedication

To my talented, organized, and caring Virgo friends,
Michael, Claire, and Kathleen, with appreciation.

CONTENTS

Acknowledgments

I would like to thank Karen Cooper and everyone at Adams Media who helped with this book. To Brendan O'Neill, Katie Corcoran Lytle, Sarah Doughty, Eileen Mullan, Casey Ebert, Sylvia Davis, and everyone else who worked on the manuscripts. To Frank Rivera, Colleen Cunningham, and Katrina Machado for their work on the book's cover and interior design. I appreciated your team spirit and eagerness to dive into the riches of astrology.

Introduction

It's time for you to have a little *"me" time*—powered by the zodiac. By tapping into your Sun sign's astrological and elemental energies, *The Little Book of Self-Care for Virgo* brings star-powered strength and cosmic relief to your life with self-care guidance tailored specifically for you.

While you may enjoy analyzing everything, Virgo, this book focuses on stepping back and taking care of your true self. This book provides information on how to incorporate self-care into your life while teaching you just how important astrology is to your overall self-care routine. You'll learn more about yourself as you learn about your sign and its governing element, earth. Then you can relax, rejuvenate, and stay balanced with more than one hundred self-care ideas and activities perfect for your Virgo personality.

From cultivating an indoor herb garden to taking a mental health day, you will find plenty of ways to heal your mind, body, and active spirit. Now, let the stars be your self-care guide!

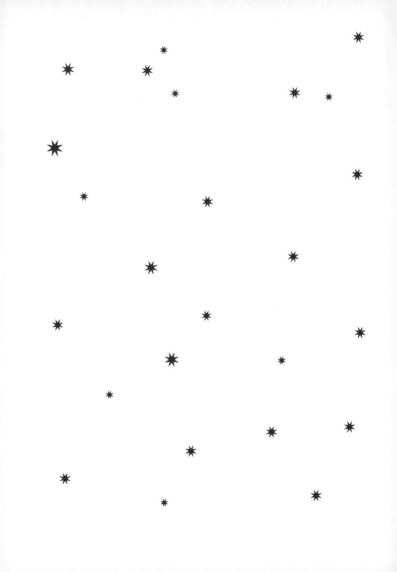

PART 1

SIGNS, ELEMENTS, AND SELF-CARE

CHAPTER 1

WHAT IS SELF-CARE?

✶

Astrology gives insights into whom to love, when to charge forward into new beginnings, and how to succeed in whatever you put your mind to. When paired with self-care, astrology can also help you relax and reclaim that part of yourself that tends to get lost in the bustle of the day. In this chapter you'll learn what self-care is—for you. (No matter your sign, self-care is more than just lit candles and quiet reflection, though these activities may certainly help you find the renewal that you seek.) You'll also learn how making a priority of personalized self-care activities can benefit you in ways you may not even have thought of. Whether you're a Virgo, a Pisces, or a Taurus, you deserve rejuvenation and renewal that's customized to your sign—this chapter reveals where to begin.

What Self-Care Is

Self-care is any activity that you do to take care of yourself. It rejuvenates your body, refreshes your mind, or realigns your spirit. It relaxes and refuels you. It gets you ready for a new day or a fresh start. It's the practices, rituals, and meaningful activities that you do, just for you, that help you feel safe, grounded, happy, and fulfilled.

The activities that qualify as self-care are amazingly unique and personalized to who you are, what you like, and, in large part, what your astrological sign is. If you're asking questions about what self-care practices are best for those ruled by earth and born under the analytical eye of Virgo, you'll find answers—and restoration—in Part 2. But, no matter which of those self-care activities speak to you and your unique place in the universe on any given day, it will fall into one of the following self-care categories—each of which pertains to a different aspect of your life:

* Physical self-care
* Emotional self-care
* Social self-care
* Mental self-care
* Spiritual self-care
* Practical self-care

When you practice all of these unique types of self-care—and prioritize your practice to ensure you are choosing the best options for your unique sign and governing element—know that you are actively working to create the version of yourself that the universe intends you to be.

Physical Self-Care

When you practice physical self-care, you make the decision to look after and restore the one physical body that has been bestowed upon you. Care for it. Use it in the best way you can imagine, for that is what the universe wishes you to do. You can't light the world on fire or move mountains if you're not doing everything you can to take care of your physical health.

Emotional Self-Care

Emotional self-care is done when you take the time to acknowledge and care for your inner self, your emotional well-being. Whether you're angry or frustrated, happy or joyful, or somewhere in between, emotional self-care happens when you choose to sit with your emotions: when you step away from the noise of daily life that often drowns out or tamps down your authentic self. Emotional self-care lets you see your inner you as the cosmos intend. Once you identify your true emotions, you can either accept them and continue to move forward on your journey or you can try to change any negative emotions for the better. The more you acknowledge your feelings and practice emotional self-care, the more you'll feel the positivity that the universe and your life holds for you.

Social Self-Care

You practice social self-care when you nurture your relationships with others, be they friends, coworkers, or family members. In today's hectic world it's easy to let relationships fall to the wayside, but it's so important to share your life with others—and let others share their lives with you. Social self-care is reciprocal and often karmic. The support and love that you put out into the universe through social self-care is given back to you by those you socialize with—often tenfold.

Mental Self-Care

Mental self-care is anything that keeps your mind working quickly and critically. It helps you cut through the fog of the day, week, or year and ensures that your quick wit and sharp mind are intact and working the way the cosmos intended. Making sure your mind is fit helps you problem-solve, decreases stress since you're not feeling overwhelmed, and keeps you feeling on top of your mental game—no matter your sign or your situation.

Spiritual Self-Care

Spiritual self-care is self-care that allows you to tap into your soul and the soul of the universe and uncover its secrets. Rather than focusing on a particular religion or set of religious beliefs, these types of self-care activities reconnect you with a higher power: the sense that something out there is bigger than you. When you meditate, you connect. When you pray, you connect. Whenever you do something that allows you to experience and marry yourself to the vastness that is the cosmos, you practice spiritual self-care.

Practical Self-Care

Self-care is what you do to take care of yourself, and practical self-care, while not as expansive as the other types, is made up of the seemingly small day-to-day tasks that bring you peace and accomplishment. These practical self-care rituals are important, but are often overlooked. Scheduling a doctor's appointment that you've been putting off is practical self-care. Getting your hair cut is practical self-care. Anything you can check off your list of things to be accomplished gives you a sacred space to breathe and allows the universe more room to bring a beautiful sense of cosmic fulfillment your way.

What Self-Care Isn't

Self-care is restorative. Self-care is clarifying. Self-care is whatever you need to do to make yourself feel secure in the universe.

Now that you know what self-care is, it's also important that you're able to see what self-care isn't. Self-care is not something that you force yourself to do because you think it will be good for you. Some signs are energy in motion and sitting still goes against their place in the universe. Those signs won't feel refreshed by lying in a hammock or sitting down to meditate. Other signs aren't able to ground themselves unless they've found a self-care practice that protects their cosmic need for peace and quiet. Those signs won't find parties, concerts, and loud venues soothing or satisfying. If a certain ritual doesn't bring you peace, clarity, or satisfaction, then it's not right for your sign and you should find something that speaks to you more clearly.

There's a difference though between not finding satisfaction in a ritual that you've tried and not wanting to try a self-care activity because you're tired or stuck in a comfort zone. Sometimes going to the gym or meeting up with friends is the self-care practice that you need to experience—whether engaging in it feels like a downer or not. So consider how you feel when you're actually doing the activity. If it feels invigorating to get on the treadmill or you feel delight when you actually catch up with your friend, the ritual is doing what it should be doing and clearing space for you—among other benefits...

The Benefits of Self-Care

The benefits of self-care are boundless and there's none that's superior to helping you put rituals in place to feel more at home in your body, in your spirit, and in your unique home in the cosmos. There are, however, other benefits to engaging in the practice of self-care that you should know.

Rejuvenates Your Immune System

No matter which rituals are designated for you by the stars, your sign, and its governing element, self-care helps both your body and mind rest, relax, and recuperate. The practice of self-care activates the parasympathetic nervous system (often called the rest and digest system), which slows your heart rate, calms the body, and overall helps your body relax and release tension. This act of decompression gives your body the space it needs to build up and strengthen your immune system, which protects you from illness.

Helps You Reconnect—with Yourself

When you practice the ritual of self-care—especially when you customize this practice based on your personal sign and governing element—you learn what you like to do and what you need to do to replenish yourself. Knowing yourself better, and allowing yourself the time and space that you need to focus on your personal needs and desires, gives you the gifts of self-confidence and self-knowledge. Setting time aside to focus on your needs also helps you put busy, must-do things aside, which gives you time to reconnect with yourself and who you are deep inside.

Increases Compassion

Perhaps one of the most important benefits of creating a self-care ritual is that, by focusing on yourself, you become more compassionate to others as well. When you truly take the time to care for yourself and make yourself and your importance in the universe a priority in your own life, you're then able to care for others and see their needs and desires in a new way. You can't pour from an empty dipper, and self-care allows you the space and clarity to do what you can to send compassion out into the world.

Starting a Self-Care Routine

Self-care should be treated as a ritual in your life, something you make the time to pause for, no matter what. You are important. You deserve rejuvenation and a sense of relaxation. You need to open your soul to the gifts that the universe is giving you, and self-care provides you with a way to ensure you're ready to receive those gifts. To begin a self-care routine, start by making yourself the priority. Do the customized rituals in Part 2 with intention, knowing the universe has already given them to you, by virtue of your sign and your governing element.

Now that you understand the role that self-care will hold in your life, let's take a closer look at the connection between self-care and astrology.

CHAPTER 2

SELF-CARE AND ASTROLOGY

✳

Astrology is the study of the connection between the objects in the heavens (the planets, the stars) and what happens here on earth. Just as the movements of the planets and other heavenly bodies influence the ebb and flow of the tides, so do they influence you—your body, your mind, your spirit. This relationship is ever present and is never more important—or personal—than when viewed through the lens of self-care.

In this chapter you'll learn how the locations of these celestial bodies at the time of your birth affect you and define the self-care activities that will speak directly to you as a Virgo, a Leo, a Capricorn, or any of the other zodiac signs. You'll see how the zodiac influences every part of your being and why ignoring its lessons can leave you feeling frustrated and unfulfilled. You'll also realize that, when you perform the rituals of self-care based on your sign, the wisdom of the cosmos will lead you down a path of fulfillment and restoration—to the return of who you really are, deep inside.

Zodiac Polarities

In astrology, all signs are mirrored by other signs that are on the opposite side of the zodiac. This polarity ensures that the zodiac is balanced and continues to flow with an unbreakable, even stream of energy. There are two different polarities in the zodiac and each is called by a number of different names:

* Yang/masculine/positive polarity
* Yin/feminine/negative polarity

Each polar opposite embodies a number of opposing traits, qualities, and attributes that will influence which self-care practices will work for or against your sign and your own personal sense of cosmic balance.

Yang

Whether male or female, those who fall under yang, or masculine, signs are extroverted and radiate their energy outward. They are spontaneous, active, bold, and fearless. They move forward in life with the desire to enjoy everything the world has to offer to them, and they work hard to transfer their inspiration and positivity to others so that those individuals may experience the same gifts that the universe offers them. All signs governed by the fire and air elements are yang and hold the potential for these dominant qualities. We will refer to them with masculine pronouns. These signs are:

* Aries
* Leo
* Sagittarius
* Gemini
* Libra
* Aquarius

There are people who hold yang energy who are introverted and retiring. However, by practicing self-care that is customized for your sign and understanding the potential ways to use your energy, you can find a way—perhaps one that's unique to you—to claim your native buoyancy and dominance and engage with the path that the universe opens for you.

Yin

Whether male or female, those who fall under yin, or feminine, signs are introverted and radiate inwardly. They draw people and experiences to them rather than seeking people and experiences in an extroverted way. They move forward in life with an energy that is reflective, receptive, and focused on communication and achieving shared goals. All signs governed by the earth and water elements are yin and hold the potential for these reflective qualities. We will refer to them with feminine pronouns. These signs are:

* Taurus
* Virgo
* Capricorn
* Cancer
* Scorpio
* Pisces

As there are people with yang energy who are introverted and retiring, there are also people with yin energy who are outgoing and extroverted. And by practicing self-care rituals that speak to your particular sign, energy, and governing body, you will reveal your true self and the balance of energy will be maintained.

Governing Elements

Each astrological sign has a governing element that defines their energy orientation and influences both the way the sign moves through the universe and relates to self-care. The elements are fire, earth, air, and water. All these signs in each element share certain characteristics, along with having their own sign-specific qualities:

* **Fire:** Fire signs are adventurous, bold, and energetic. They enjoy the heat and warm environments and look to the sun and fire as a means to recharge their depleted batteries. They're competitive, outgoing, and passionate. The fire signs are Aries, Leo, and Sagittarius.
* **Earth:** Earth signs all share a common love and tendency toward a practical, material, sensual, and economic orientation. The earth signs are Taurus, Virgo, and Capricorn.
* **Air:** Air is the most ephemeral element and those born under this element are thinkers, innovators, and communicators. The air signs are Gemini, Libra, and Aquarius.
* **Water:** Water signs are instinctual, compassionate, sensitive, and emotional. The water signs are Cancer, Scorpio, and Pisces.

Chapter 3 teaches you all about the ways your specific governing element influences and drives your connection to your cosmically chosen self-care rituals, but it's important that you realize how important these elemental traits are to your self-care practice and to the activities that will help restore and reveal your true self.

Sign Qualities

Each of the astrological elements governs three signs. Each of these three signs is also given its own quality or mode, which corresponds to a different part of each season: the beginning, the middle, or the end.

*   **Cardinal signs:** The cardinal signs initiate and lead in each season. Like something that is just starting out, they are actionable, enterprising, and assertive, and are born leaders. The cardinal signs are Aries, Cancer, Libra, and Capricorn.
*   **Fixed signs:** The fixed signs come into play when the season is well established. They are definite, consistent, reliable, motivated by principles, and powerfully stubborn. The fixed signs are Taurus, Leo, Scorpio, and Aquarius.
*   **Mutable signs:** The mutable signs come to the forefront when the seasons are changing. They are part of one season, but also part of the next. They are adaptable, versatile, and flexible. The mutable signs are Gemini, Virgo, Sagittarius, and Pisces.

Each of these qualities tells you a lot about yourself and who you are. They also give you invaluable information about the types of self-care rituals that your sign will find the most intuitive and helpful.

Ruling Planets

In addition to qualities and elements, each specific sign is ruled by a particular planet that lends its personality to those born under that sign. Again, these sign-specific traits give you valuable insight into the personality of the signs and the self-care rituals that may best rejuvenate them. The signs that correspond to each planet—and the ways that those planetary influences determine your self-care options—are as follows:

* **Aries:** Ruled by Mars, Aries is passionate, energetic, and determined.
* **Taurus:** Ruled by Venus, Taurus is sensual, romantic, and fertile.
* **Gemini:** Ruled by Mercury, Gemini is intellectual, changeable, and talkative.
* **Cancer:** Ruled by the Moon, Cancer is nostalgic, emotional, and home loving.
* **Leo:** Ruled by the Sun, Leo is fiery, dramatic, and confident.
* **Virgo:** Ruled by Mercury, Virgo is intellectual, analytical, and responsive.
* **Libra:** Ruled by Venus, Libra is beautiful, romantic, and graceful.
* **Scorpio:** Ruled by Mars and Pluto, Scorpio is intense, powerful, and magnetic.
* **Sagittarius:** Ruled by Jupiter, Sagittarius is optimistic, boundless, and larger than life.
* **Capricorn:** Ruled by Saturn, Capricorn is wise, patient, and disciplined.

* **Aquarius:** Ruled by Uranus, Aquarius is independent, unique, and eccentric.
* **Pisces:** Ruled by Neptune and Jupiter, Pisces is dreamy, sympathetic, and idealistic.

A Word on Sun Signs

When someone is a Virgo, Leo, Sagittarius, or any of the other zodiac signs, it means that the sun was positioned in this constellation in the heavens when they were born. Your Sun sign is a dominant factor in defining your personality, your best self-care practices, and your soul nature. Every person also has the position of the Moon, Mercury, Venus, Mars, Jupiter, Saturn, Uranus, Neptune, and Pluto. These planets can be in any of the elements: fire signs, earth signs, air signs, or water signs. If you have your entire chart calculated by an astrologer or on an Internet site, you can see the whole picture and learn about all your elements. Someone born under Leo with many signs in another element will not be as concentrated in the fire element as someone with five or six planets in Leo. Someone born in Pisces with many signs in another element will not be as concentrated in the water element as someone with five or six panets in Pisces. And so on. Astrology is a complex system and has many shades of meaning. For our purposes, looking at the self-care practices designated by your Sun sign, or what most people consider *their* sign, will give you the information you need to move forward and find fulfillment and restoration.

ESSENTIAL ELEMENTS: EARTH

✳

The earth element is most familiar to all of us, for the earth is our home. We are born on this planet and are the custodians of her beauty, natural resources, health, and well-being. There is an intimate connection between human beings and the balance of the earth's conditions. The earth signs (Taurus, Virgo, and Capricorn) feel this connection more than other signs, and their approach to self-care reflects their relationship with this natural element. They are practical and realistic, and they need self-care techniques that match their disposition. More so, earth signs are rooted in the material, physical world. They are, at their best, pragmatic, sensual, patient, and grounded. At their worst they can be greedy, lascivious, and materialistic.

Most humans face the polarity of balancing the need and competition of making a living, with the dreams and desires of their heart. Earth signs accept this as reality instead of fighting against it. Becoming successful in the material world is their natural inclination. Any self-care they do must reflect that ultimate goal as well. Let's take a look at the mythological importance of the earth and its counterparts, the basic characteristics of the three earth signs, and what they all have in common when it comes to self-care.

The Mythology of Earth

There are many creation myths from all over the world. Most of these myths feature a Mother Earth figure. In Greek mythology, which forms the basis for much of astrology, Gaia was the Earth Mother. She represented the circle of life. Gaia came out of chaos and gave birth to Ouranos, the sky god, who also happened to be her husband. (The Greeks liked to keep things in the family.) The relationship between Gaia and Ouranos was so passionate that their children could not emerge from Gaia's womb. One of these unborn children was Cronos who in Roman astrology was called Saturn. Cronos decided to overthrow Ouranos and in the womb emasculated his father. And the sky separated from the earth. Cronos, the lord of time, ruled the universe for a time but later got his comeuppance as Zeus/Jupiter displaced him and became the chief god and ruler of all. These myths regarding the separation of earth and sky (or heaven and earth) abound in ancient world cultures.

Earth signs strive for measured success, and often seek worldly possessions to solidify their self-worth. This need for stability is indicative of their element. Earth, after all, is the foundation for life. It is tangible, solid, and defined. Many earth signs are so grounded in reality they can lose track of their emotional well-being. Self-care rituals that cater to both mind and soul are key for earth signs. Simplicity and practicality are often paramount.

The Element of Earth

Earth signs are known for their measured approach to life. They are typically patient, reliable, and disciplined, traits that often lead to prosperity. Because of this, earth signs are often viewed as well balanced and levelheaded, hence the saying *down-to-earth*. Earth signs are known as the sensible, pragmatic signs, choosing to focus on practical solutions over emotions. They are not light and buoyant like air signs, passionate and fiery like fire signs, nor empathetic and fluid like water signs. Instead, they are committed, strong, and trustworthy. For example, Taurus is loyal and always ready to help friends and family in need. Virgo is hardworking and will never back down from a challenge. And Capricorn is responsible and will help others stick to their responsibilities as well.

Astrological Symbols

The astrological symbols (also called the zodiacal symbols) of the earth signs also give you hints as to how earth signs move through the world. Each symbol ties back to the nature associated with earth signs:

* Taurus is the Bull
* Virgo is the Maiden gathering the harvest
* Capricorn is the Goat

All these signs show steadfast and intimate harmony with the cycles of the seasons and a personal connection with the earth: the meadows, green fields, and rocks. Taurus comes from ancient myths about the cults that worshipped the bull as a fertility symbol. She represents coiled power not yet unleashed. Virgo is the only earth sign that has a human symbol. She is a mutable sign and like a junior Mother Earth. Capricorn is of the earth but climbs the mountains of ambition and spiritual ascent. Each earth sign's personality and subsequent approach to self-care connect to the qualities of these representative symbols.

Signs and Seasonal Modes

Each of the elements in astrology also has a sign that corresponds to a different part of each season.

* **Fixed:** Taurus, the first earth sign, comes when spring is in full bloom. Taurus is called a fixed earth sign because she comes when the season is well established. The fixed signs are definite, motivated by principles, and powerfully stubborn.
* **Mutable:** Virgo, the second earth sign, moves us from summer to autumn. These signs are called mutable. In terms of character the mutable signs are changeable and flexible.
* **Cardinal:** Capricorn is the leader of the earth signs because she marks the beginning of winter and the time around the winter solstice.

If you know your element and whether you are a cardinal, fixed, or mutable sign, you know a lot about yourself. This is invaluable for self-care and is reflected in the customized earth sign self-care rituals found in Part 2.

Earth Signs and Self-Care

The earth signs' first motivation in life is to feel comfortable in their physical surroundings. For physical self-care their most important motivation is routine and diligence. Earth signs don't require a lot of variety. Their motto is, "If something works, keep it." The downside to this attitude is that earth signs can get stuck in a rut, but the benefits of continuous physical exercise, self-care, and good diet at all ages are the cornerstones of comfort for earth signs.

You may notice that earth signs touch other people more frequently than other elements do. They pat, reach out, hug, and extend themselves physically to others. They also have an intimate and close sense of personal space and will be upfront and personal in encountering new people or old friends. They want and need to sense the whole person.

Earth signs take self-care actions in a very practical way. For example, if an earth sign wants to exercise more, they may think the following: "If I can exercise more, I will lose weight and be healthier, so I will have more years to build my business, enjoy my family, and do what I want."

Spiritually, earth signs feel little division between body and soul. If they feel comfortable and well physically, then their soul qualities can evolve and blossom. Some people may feel that the high-minded notion of spiritual retreat and meditation defines a spiritual person, and they therefore look down on an earth sign's practical thoughts, such as "How much will it cost to go on this retreat and how much time will it take?" Earth signs don't consider this to be materialism at the expense of spirituality. Instead, to them, it is a clear recognition of the practical and sensible way the world works. Ashrams, well-being programs, herbs, and health practices cost money, and it is a reasonable question to ask if the practice is worth it.

The most important "rule" for earth signs is that self-care feed the senses. Whatever the plan is, it should include every sense. The activity must look appealing, smell good, taste good, sound good, and feel good. The more all the senses are involved, the happier the earth signs will be and the more likely they will be to follow the program. If the price is reasonable, so much the better. But too much sensual input can cause earth signs to overindulge and become lethargic. This is a potential pitfall for all the earth signs.

The overall purpose and meaning of the earth signs is to offer practical solutions to maintain personal self-care and the health of the planet. The earth signs have a lot to teach the people around them. Modern life is increasingly jagged. The earth signs demonstrate the value of solid measured progress. Walk don't run, and take things as they come. This attitude can preserve each of us as well as planet earth.

So now that you know what earth signs need to practice self-care, let's look at each of the pragmatic characteristics of Virgo and how she can maintain her inner balance.

CHAPTER 4

SELF-CARE FOR VIRGO

✳

Dates: August 23–September 22
Element: Earth
Polarity: Yin
Quality: Mutable
Symbol: Maiden
Ruler: Mercury

Virgo is the second earth sign, and her ruler is the planet Mercury. She is mutable, or changeable, and ushers us from summer to autumn. The mutable signs come at the end of a season and move us into the next season. Virgo is also the last of the personality signs of the zodiac.

Virgo represents the seed planted in the earth that must take root and grow toward the light. Beginning with Aries and ending with Virgo, the soul's journey is to develop internal personality characteristics.

After Virgo, the remaining signs of the zodiac evolve from the personality to soul growth through relationships.

Virgo is also the sign of service to others. She gathers information and analyzes what she needs to know for herself and others. The essential nature of Virgo is to search for synthesis and wholeness, and the most valuable quality in this search is Virgo's capacity for analysis. When she uses her analyzing skills in service to herself or others in work, Virgo is balanced. When she criticizes herself and others, she becomes nervously irritable and impossible to please. This critical faculty also cuts off her creativity and leaves a fussy agitation that does not serve her well. Additionally, if Virgo relies exclusively on her critical and analytical faculties, she can become so bogged down in details that she misses the forest for the trees.

Virgo's mission in terms of personality development is the quest for perfection. Virgo wants to get everything just right. But the important word is *quest*, not perfection. In the Middle East a handwoven carpet always contains a flaw, because the weavers believe that only God can create something perfect. Virgo's quest carries her through her life, minding details and working hard. After all, if she achieves perfection, she will have nothing left to do!

The symbol for Virgo is the Maiden holding sheaves of wheat from the harvest. The symbol harkens back to the Babylonian goddess of fertility, Ishtar. In Greek mythology the harvest maiden was associated with Persephone, the earth goddess Demeter's daughter. Hades abducted Persephone and took her to the underworld. In despair, her mother forbade the earth to be fruitful during the six months of her daughter's captivity; these were the winter months. When Persephone emerged from the underworld, the next months were bountiful and fruitful. Hence, Virgo's association with the harvest.

Self-Care and Virgo

Self-care for Virgo comes naturally. She has jittery nerves and is very sensitive, and oftentimes these nerves create health concerns, so she makes sure that she takes care of herself in every way possible. She usually follows conventional medicine but also has a talent for exploring alternative medicine. Like her mythical ancestor Demeter, she has an intuitive understanding of herbs and is familiar with the subtle effects of essential oils. When Virgo is in balance, her body serves her and her work; when she is not, she can be a hypochondriac and run from doctor to doctor seeking cures. The best self-care program for Virgo is to follow regular checkups and then let health concerns go. If Virgo tunes in to her body, she will know what to do. If she is in a mental whirl, then no cure or medicine can calm her.

Mercury, Virgo's ruling planet, rules the mind and communication. This association serves Virgo when she is gathering information, because her mind is quick to make connections. When Mercury spins his whirl of mental preoccupations, however, Virgo can get lost in the details and her mind cannot relax. Every bit of information becomes the thing that will cure, or the therapy that is necessary, or the medicine that will help. Usually this is a panicky reaction and nothing resolves itself until the mind calms down.

Virgo Rules the Intestines

The area of the body ruled by Virgo is the intestines. Physically, these are the organs of the body responsible for digestion and assimilation of food, and, metaphysically, for processing experiences and emotions. The intestines are highly sensitive in Virgo and the first place to attend to for self-care is digestive health.

Virgo can have allergies that come and go, as well as food sensitivities. A Virgo child may be a picky eater from a young age, and parents need to introduce a variety of foods early so that the child learns that there are many eating possibilities. Also, Virgo of any age may eat the same food for weeks or months and then tire of it. This is a natural rhythm to give the body what it needs. Junk food is never a good idea for Virgo; however, as an earth sign, she may indulge in comfort food every so often. She usually does not like spicy food or exotic dishes. The more Virgo follows her own senses toward what she eats and doesn't eat, the better she will feel.

Self-care in exercise for Virgo is relatively simple. She likes sports that don't involve a lot of equipment or fuss: going for a jog, playing a game of tennis, swimming laps, and dancing. Some Virgos love the elegance of ballroom dancing and the tango. Running track and graceful martial arts are also great sports for Virgo.

Competition with others is not usually Virgo's style. She is content to play and feel good in her physical self. Usually Virgo's muscles are not physically dense, so stretching and easy warm-ups are essential to staying injury-free. The primary goal in sports for Virgo is getting away from mental preoccupations.

Psychologically, Virgo needs a counselor to speak to, if only to sort out all the thoughts in her mind. She has no problem exploring her motivations and is eager to gain knowledge about why she may think the way she does—however, Virgo is not an emotional sign. Therapy is for the purpose of gaining insight and knowledge. This process may not unleash emotional clarity, but it will settle her very active brain and give her tools to help in life. Cognitive therapy or hypnotherapy can be very effective for Virgo. Hypnotherapy speaks to the unconscious and can help Virgo relax. Also, hypnotherapy is useful if Virgo has a problem or phobia—it will help clear out the mental debris that is getting in the way of moving past the issue. It may take practice, but Virgo likes working toward a goal.

One of Virgo's finest qualities is the desire to help and serve others. Virgo wants to keep helping, but if her helpfulness is not balanced with self-care, she can tire herself out quickly. The first rule of serving and helping others for everyone is to keep renewing your own energy.

Underlying all the digging for information and efforts that Virgo extends toward her self-care is a desire to be of service to others. This is the part of the personality that Virgo is developing. A prime example was fellow Virgo Mother Teresa. She served with no thought of her own well-being. Of course, she was a saint, but every Virgo has a kernel of this quest to help and comfort others. A motivating factor for her in all self-care is to be well and comfortable in mind and body so that Virgo can serve through work, and through her relationships with family, friends, and neighbors.

When working to serve, Virgo is blessed with an easy optimism and a formidable ability to organize anything. She rarely has enemies and her fastidiousness can be a model for "how to get things done." We all benefit from Virgo's desire to help and serve.

Virgo and Self-Care Success

Since Virgo is "preprogrammed" to be sensitive to her body and mind's needs, success in self-care is a matter of following the rules. She loves to check things off the list. Physical, done;

eating plan, done; massage, done. All these activities help Virgo achieve her goals and improve her well-being. She likes to have fun, but taking care of the details of self-care is more important. Counting is the best approach for success. Virgo wants to know her statistics exactly: what is her blood pressure, how many steps, how many pounds, and what exactly is the problem. She loves to plan exactly how she will go about implementing and improving her self-care actions.

Some pitfalls to success for Virgo are frustration and fear that her plan is not working. She is not impatient per se, but needs to feel assured that her health and life efforts are working. If the problem is illness, she needs to have confidence that the medical professionals are on her side and doing their best. She measures her success and when she sees progress, her mind relaxes and healing can happen.

With the rulership of quick-thinking Mercury, boredom can be another pitfall for Virgo. If an activity becomes routine and Virgo is just going through the motions, she will feel rigid and not comforted by the regular rhythm of her plan. That is the time to change things up. As a mutable sign Virgo is not usually rigid, but if the "to-do list" takes over and she loses confidence in her activities, then she needs a new plan.

Virgo can become overworked and overdo anything. If she gathers too much information or has too many "must dos," paralysis sets in and she cannot see a clear way to proceed. Internet research fosters this overwhelming feeling. It is best for Virgo to speak to professionals rather than dive into chat groups on the Internet.

With Virgo's essential nature in mind, let's take a look at some rituals that will help her in her quest.

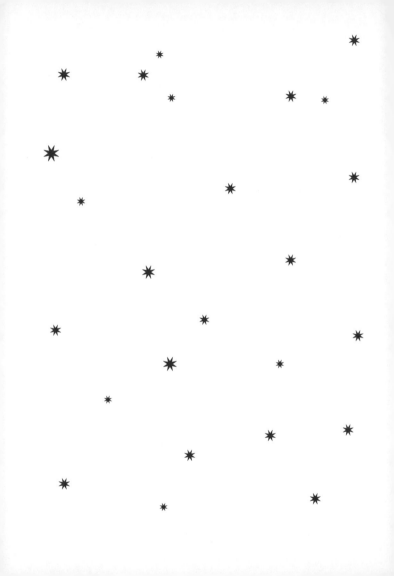

♍

PART 2

SELF-CARE
RITUALS
— FOR —
VIRGO

Break Free from Your Comfort Zone

As an earth sign, you tend to be organized, ritualistic, and highly structured. However, because you like structure and rituals so much, you can easily fall into repeating patterns, and even if that pattern is not particularly healthy, you'll stay with it. Once you're in a comfortable place, it's hard for you to change your habits. But being afraid to change something can hold you back from making life-changing decisions or improving yourself. Getting out of your regular rituals will boost your confidence and open up new doors in your life. Make a choice to break out of your routine and try something new.

Concentrate on the Exhale

A s a hardworking Virgo your mind is always busy thinking about your next task. Your dedication is admirable, but you should also work in several breaks throughout your day to quiet and clear your mind. Slow the racing thoughts with a meditation during which you focus on exhaling.

Exhaling is actually a key part of reducing stress and promoting relaxation. Many of us can master the art of breathing *in* slowly, but then we tend to force air *out* in a hurry. In your daily breaks, breathe in slowly, counting the seconds, and then try to exhale for the same amount of time. If your exhale is shorter, try with each breath to extend it a bit longer. As you breathe, imagine yourself in your favorite relaxation spot. Take these breaks at least three times during your workday (set a timer on your phone to remind yourself), and then once again before bedtime.

Don't Worry Too Much about Your Health

I t's a great goal to want to be healthy. But Virgo can sometimes take that goal to an extreme and stress far too much about her health, fretting about every ache and pain and committing to adopt every new health-food fad.

You'd be much better served by simply eating well, visiting your doctor for regular checkups, and getting quality sleep—then letting go so the universe can take care of the rest. Remind yourself how hard you work on your health, and when you feel particularly worried, practice some deep breathing as you visualize yourself in a healthy, strong, happy state. You can also repeat a mantra like "I am well" to yourself to reinforce the feeling and dispel the fear.

Work Through Tummy Troubles

Virgo rules the intestines, which means that you might experience digestive issues more frequently than other signs do. Luckily, these issues are often just the result of excessive worry and not a serious medical problem.

If your digestive system isn't cooperating, visit the doctor to rule out an infection, and then try to pinpoint what concern might be causing the discomfort. Are you worried about a big work project, an upcoming move, or a particularly large credit card bill? If so, try to break the problem down into small parts and tackle it bit by bit. Addressing the root cause of your stress may well alleviate your tummy troubles as well.

Get Stepping

In terms of fitness, earth signs like measurable results. They like to be able to calculate situations and use concrete facts to do so. This is why a pedometer, smart watch, or fitness tracker would be perfect for you. You like to be able to know the exact number of steps you have taken so you can use that information to plan, to calculate further exercise or meals, or as a motivator for yourself. Those folks who go willy-nilly into exercise are not for you; hard facts and organization will get the job done for an earth sign.

Try a Colorful Meditation

Meditation is a great way for Virgo to cleanse her mind of worries and recharge her batteries. But it can be a challenge to clear her mind for very long with so many thoughts running through her brain!

Try this color meditation to give yourself something specific to think about. The colors white and yellow are particularly powerful for Virgo—yellow represents optimism and energy, while white represents protection and goodness. You can either imagine orbs of soothing white or yellow light, or visualize relaxing images, such as a field of yellow sunflowers or the white sands of an empty beach. Feel your connection to nature and the colors as you breathe slowly.

Eat What You Love

Earth signs love their foods, and they especially like to be relaxed and savor their food when they eat it. However, many earth signs have sensitive palates and have to be choosey about what they eat. You need to listen to your body about what it needs and what it can tolerate, and when you find a food you like, enjoy it! Also, being conscious about what foods you are putting in your body is important for earth signs. When you can, try to choose foods grown without pesticides, added hormones, or artificial fertilizers as many of these things can irritate your body. Go with natural and organic versions of the foods you love.

Go for a Jog

E xercise is essential for Virgo, both for its many physical benefits and its ability to clear her busy mind. While there are countless exercise options out there, sometimes a simple jog is the best idea for you.

Jogging is both inexpensive and easy to do anywhere, inside on a treadmill or outside on trails or sidewalks, and you can make each jog different by trying these ideas: vary your route so you see different areas of your neighborhood or town, create several playlists so you can listen to music that matches your mood, and revamp your workout wardrobe so that you look and feel your best every time.

Record Your Self-Care

Virgo has excellent attention to detail and is a wonderful record keeper. You might employ those skills at work or with your financial business, but why not apply it to something fun too—like your self-care?

As you know, the benefits of self-care are more strongly felt if you make them a habit. So keep track of your self-care by noting what you've done on your smartphone or tablet, or through another type of online app. You can even go back to basics and jot everything down in a notebook or dedicated self-care journal. Chart your progress, your highs and lows, and make note of any upcoming goals you'd like to achieve. Review your progress periodically and make adjustments as needed. Keeping track of your self-care will help keep you motivated and engaged.

Heal Your Spirit with a Garden

Y ou are an earth sign, after all. What could be more in tune with your nature than to work with the earth? As an earth sign, you tend to hold on to stress and have trouble releasing it, but working with the soil will bring you into a state of calmness. When you are connected to an element, just being near it and working with it can help realign your energy and bring peace.

So go out and till your soil, buy seeds or plants, and then plant them in precise and organized rows. As you watch your plants grow and tend to them, you will discover your stress will wash away. Even if you don't have space to plant a garden where you live, just getting your hands in the soil will help heal your spirit.

Play Individual Sports

————————

Virgo loves to be active, and while earth signs find team sports like volleyball and soccer appealing, Virgo's standards for excellence are high, and she might not enjoy having her fate in others' hands some of the time.

This makes individual sports like tennis, golf, and skiing a great fit. You'll get a great workout (especially if you skip the golf cart!), but can play at your pace, and in your own style. You can also use your time spent on the links, hills, or court to clear worries out of your busy mind. These individual sports require intense focus; you can't perfect your serve while practicing next week's board presentation or hit a putt while mentally assessing your bank account.

Use a Scent Diffuser

—————————

Savoring calming scents is a great way to engage your sense of smell during the relaxation process. When you need to unwind after a busy day, turn to a scent diffuser to help.

There are many types of scent diffusers, such as reed diffusers or candles, so choose one that you prefer. Then find a scent that meets your needs. Virgo rules all scents, but some fragrances that are particularly good matches are lemon verbena, jasmine, and lavender. Lemon verbena is a strong, invigorating scent that might help get you moving in the morning, while jasmine and lavender are more soothing and relaxing and better for bedtime.

Give Yourself Some Time

———————————

Earth signs are grounded, logical, and reliable, so it goes without saying that you hate to be late. In fact, punctuality is an admired quality of the earth signs. If a situation occurs that causes you to be late, it can fill you with stress and cause anxiety. So, with that in mind, make a point of giving yourself some extra time to get where you need to be. This will give a cushion in case some unexpected events pop up and delay you. You know being late will stress you out, so do your mind and spirit a favor and try to eliminate anything that might interfere with your timeliness.

Ask about Royal Jelly

E ver heard of royal jelly? It's a milky secretion produced by worker honeybees to help keep the queen healthy. Turns out, it also might help humans stay healthy as well, as it has the potential to alleviate issues related to menstruation and menopause, boost the immune system, stimulate fertility, and help to heal bone fractures.

Assuming you do not have asthma and you're not allergic to bees or bee products, ask your doctor about taking a royal jelly supplement in winter to improve your health. You can find over-the-counter capsules at your local health food store.

Organize Your Closets

———————————

Virgo is practical, logical, and neat—so organizing your closets isn't a chore for you, it's a fun activity! Even though you try to keep things tidy, every once in a while, it's a good idea to look through your closets and get them organized.

To start, sort through your belongings and get rid of anything that's not useful. Next, assess the items you're keeping and figure out what the best storage method is for them—hangers, open baskets, closed bins? If the process seems overwhelming, call in a professional organizer to lend a hand. When you're done, you'll feel productive and grateful that you have more space and a new system that works for you.

Do Some Heavy Lifting

E arth signs are incredibly strong people, mentally and physically. With that in mind, make sure you emphasize weight and strength training in your work-outs. Develop your lifting muscles by exercising with weights and concentrating on weight-bearing exercis-es throughout your life. There are so many variations of weight and strength training that you can easily find a routine that suits your age, strength, general health, and energy level. Strength training will help you fight the loss of muscle, bone mass, and strength that occurs naturally with aging. It is also great for your joints, an area of concern for a lot of earth signs.

Make Your Home on the Ground Floor

E arth signs instinctually prefer to keep their feet planted firmly on the ground—so their homes should be, as well! Creating a safe, comfortable home is important to earth signs, since it gives them a place to focus on their creative impulses and build a space that's perfect for feeling stable and reenergized.

Ground floor apartments have plenty of perks, such as access to outdoor yard spaces and easier move-in days. And better yet, you'll recharge best in a home where you can easily see (and touch!) the ground. Skip the high-rise apartment, and go for something closer to the first floor instead.

Carry Pink Jasper with You

Because they come from the earth, crystals can connect you to the planet's energy. Whether you wear them in forms of jewelry, place them around your house as décor, or meditate while holding them, gemstones have the power to improve your happiness and well-being.

Each crystal has its own unique capabilities. For Virgo the pink jasper stone is an especially powerful ally. Ranging in shades from a soft, pale pink to a rich fuchsia, pink jasper encourages grounding, Look for an unpolished stone, which has more intrinsic ener-gy. Carry a piece of it in your left pocket every day (because the left side of your body absorbs energy) to bring you comfort and peace.

Try Bach's Crab Apple Remedy

I f you're feeling out of sorts and unsure how to right yourself, you might want to consider turning to a natural remedy. One such option is the original Bach Flower Remedies, which are made from wildflowers and, according to the company, "gently restore the balance between mind and body by casting out negative emotions such as fear, worry, hatred and indecision which interfere with the equilibrium of the being as a whole."

In particular, Virgo can benefit from using the crab apple remedy, which claims to help you overcome any negative self-image issues you might have. If you find yourself critiquing your body or feeling unhappy with many things when you look in the mirror, try adding a couple of drops of crab apple remedy to a glass of water (follow the directions on the bottle) and drinking slowly. You might just find that you now see yourself with much kinder eyes. (The Bach Flower Remedies are available online.)

Take a Library-Focused Vacation

Sure, beaches, snowy mountains, and ancient cities are interesting vacation spots...but so are libraries! Why not create a trip where you visit beautiful libraries in the US and abroad? After all, since she is ruled by Mercury, the planet of communication, Virgo loves books and the written word.

You could head to the University of Oxford's stunning Bodleian reading rooms, with their rich wood finishes and leather-bound books, and check out a copy of the Gutenberg Bible. Or visit the library hall in the Clementinum in Prague, with its gilded accents and frescoed ceiling. Vancouver's Central Library is reminiscent of the Colosseum and has an open-air concourse. The Musashino Art University Museum and Library in Tokyo is actually built out of thousands of bookshelves, and simply walled in with glass. Egypt's Bibliotheca Alexandrina is an enormous circular building that also features a planetarium and museums. With options like these, you might need to plan more than one vacation!

Get Outside!

L ying on the couch after work might have become routine for you, but what if you switched your habit? Earth signs are prone to becoming lethargic, so try to get outside for a walk almost every evening after you eat.

Walking will aid digestion, help you stay fit, and encourage you to decompress and unwind in a healthy way. Vary your route periodically to keep the walk from getting boring. An evening stroll is also a great way to engage with your community—say hi to people you walk by, buy lemonade from a kids' stand, or even join in a pickup basketball game.

Detox with a Mud Mask

———————

After a long day, nothing feels better than a relaxing facial mask. And what better type for an earth sign than a mud mask? Clear away the pollutants and bacteria your face is exposed to on a daily basis using an element of the earth itself.

If time and your budget allow, you can visit a spa for a mud mask—but if that's not possible, pick one up at a drugstore or natural foods store and apply it yourself at home, taking slow, deep breaths as you let the mixture sit on your face. You'll find this detox to be especially restorative and cleansing.

Try Licorice to Calm
Your Stomach

———————

Since Virgo rules the digestive system, you might find that your stomach acts up every once in a while. Instead of reaching for your usual over-the-counter medication, ask your doctor if you can try an herb supplement that could help your gastrointestinal problems—licorice!

In its natural state (meaning, not the sugar-laden candied form you might be familiar with), licorice is packed with antioxidants that can fight infection, ease heartburn, calm ulcers, and relieve constipation. Because licorice contains a substance called glycyrrhizin, which can cause side effects, make sure to look for DGL, or deglycyrrhizinated, licorice. DGL licorice is available in a capsule supplement.

Enjoy the Power of Music

————————————

Earth signs love music. When you're feeling stressed, try using music to relax yourself. If you find yourself in a difficult situation, try to take a break to re-center and calm down. Put on your headphones, and let the sound of the music soothe you and distract you from your worries. Experiment with different genres to see what works best for you.

You may even find it relaxing to do some singing yourself—even if it's only in the safety of your own shower!

Volunteer for an Environmental Cause

Donating your time and effort to a cause you're passionate about is a great way to show you care about the world around you—and yourself. After all, research shows that people who volunteer are less stressed, have more friends, and are more confident! As an earth sign, honor your connection to the planet by volunteering for a group that protects the environment, reduces pollution, encourages people to get outside, or safeguards animals.

There are many ways to help, including performing manual labor, organizing fundraising, and offering skills like bookkeeping or web design. You will feel fulfilled and proud—and your work will be making a difference.

Use Yoga to Recharge

Working out is all about finding the right balance. Try mixing your weights and cardio with yoga stretches to keep muscles limber. Think yoga isn't right for you? Don't worry—there are many different styles and class types, so you'll be able to find the perfect, restorative approach that's right for you and your body's needs.

By adding yoga into your routine, you may find yourself becoming stronger and more flexible. But your brain will also benefit by getting a break from thinking, worrying, and stressing. Since it's important to focus your awareness on your body and concentrate on performing each pose as best you can, you'll find your worries can take a back seat while you recharge.

Live It Up on Weekdays!

There's no need to wait for a weekend to go out for dinner or a night on the town! As an earth sign, you probably enjoy structure and routine, but you don't want to fall into ruts either. To avoid that, shake things up and enjoy a concert on a Monday evening, head out to dinner at a new restaurant on a Tuesday night, or go dancing on Wednesday after work. You'll release any stress you've been holding onto and take the pressure off your weekends to supply *every* bit of fun in your life.

Become a Plant Parent

I t should come as no surprise that earth signs find it reassuring to include touches of nature in their homes. Keep yourself centered and relaxed by surrounding yourself with plants. If you're not able to live in a place with easy access to the natural world, try bringing nature to you! City dwellers can plant window boxes or fill their apartments with different types of houseplants.

A window herb garden is a great place to start. Try common herbs like basil, chives, cilantro, oregano, or parsley, which can be great additions to any meal and have many other useful qualities. (Did you know basil is a natural mosquito repellent?) Go all-natural and see how many ways your new garden can benefit your daily life!

Save Your Seat

E arth signs are known for seeking stability in their lives—and their work environment is no different. No matter your organizational style or tasks at hand, a sturdy, well-designed office chair is a must-have for any busy earth sign. It isn't easy to get through the workday if you're uncomfortable and distracted. You'll be able to stay focused and work more productively if you're settled at your desk in a chair that's comfortable for you.

Not only will you be better able to concentrate at work, you'll also be taking care of your body. No more stiff necks or backaches for you!

Indulge in Comfort Food

Craving some mac and cheese? A homemade chocolate chip cookie? Maybe even a simple, classic PB&J (peanut butter and jelly)? Reliable earth signs sometimes need to reclaim their roots and find comfort in the well known and well loved.

After a long day indulge in your love of comfort food, whether that's a cheesy slice of pepperoni pizza or a gooey brownie still warm from the oven. Take an uplifting trip down memory lane with simple foods that remind you of your childhood. Enjoyed in moderation, these treats will keep your stomach full and your heart happy.

Learn at Your Own Pace

As an earth sign, you love to learn new things and are not dissuaded when the subject seems difficult or arduous. Persistence is definitely an earth sign characteristic! But while you love to discover new skills, you don't like being monitored while you do so. You learn better while working solo and do not like to have someone looking over your shoulder. Often methodical and meticulous, you have no patience for those who want to just jump in and go with it. So don't put yourself through that! If you are part of a group for work or school, try suggesting that everyone work on ideas separately and then reconvene to discuss them. That way you can have your solo learning time while still being a team player!

Enjoy Arugula Salads

———————————

Boring iceberg lettuce salads can make anyone reluctant to reach for greens. But there's a whole world of salad greens beyond iceberg.

With Virgo's potential digestive issues, arugula is an especially good choice. Its bright, peppery flavor is anything but boring! Plus, arugula is a nutritional powerhouse—it contains fiber, potassium, calcium, magnesium, iron, folate, vitamins A, C, and K, and even protein! To complete an arugula salad, add a lemony dressing, something sweet like raisins or berries, and a freshly shredded sharp cheese. You'll find yourself looking forward to salads again!

Look Into Beekeeping

Local honey has astounding health-promoting properties—it can soothe sore throats, potentially minimize the effects of pollen and allergies, and boost your immune system. Beekeeping is also a fascinating hobby that you might want to consider.

These days it's more important than ever to promote bee health. Bees are essential to the pollination process for our natural food sources, yet recently bee populations have been sharply declining thanks to industrialized agriculture, climate change, and pesticide use. If you have the space, why not do your part for the earth and your own health and keep a beehive in your own yard? Visit a site like www.beebuilt.com, and contact a local beekeeping organization for information on buying equipment and protective clothing, educating yourself, and starting a hive.

Find Balance for
Your Finances

Self-care isn't always about having fun—sometimes it's simply about that sense of accomplishment you get from checking off a task on your to-do list. Perfect for practical earth signs, make sure to get through those financial day-to-day activities, like reviewing your budget or balancing your checkbook.

Earth signs can be cautious and like to have a sense of security, instead of taking unnecessary risks. A balanced earth sign is able to successfully manage their cautious tendencies and their indulgences. That careful decision-making can help you manage your money well; earth signs have a natural awareness that helps them judge their financial situation exactly. Just make sure you're not obsessing over the task!

Keep Some Toys on Your Desk

———————

Virgo is a hard worker, which is great for your productivity levels and career success. But, sometimes, you need to take a break and lower your intensity a bit so you don't burn out.

In the middle of a busy workday, it can be difficult to remember to relax—so put some toys or interactive elements on your desk to remind yourself. Whether it's an old-fashioned Slinky, a soothing Zen sand and rock garden, or a place to doodle (like an Etch A Sketch or a whiteboard with colored pens), these items can invite you and your colleagues to clear your mind while keeping your hands busy. Plus, they're just plain fun!

Create the Perfect Work Space

You probably spend a good chunk of your day at your workstation. But if it's cluttered and almost every surface is covered with paper or folders—and you can't ever find a pen that works—it's time to reevaluate how things are set up.

Virgo appreciates any form and function that works for her. Apply that theme to your work desk and purchase some paper trays or vertical organizers for your folders, a sturdy cup for pens, and a desk drawer divider for paper clips and extra staples. Then choose various colored sticky notes that can represent different parts of your job or home responsibilities. The different colors will help you see quickly what area needs the most attention.

Hold High Tea

Virgo appreciates the proper ritual of high tea: the crisp linen tablecloth, the perfectly folded napkins, the spotless bone china cups, the polished silver spoons, the tasteful floral centerpiece, and the perfectly arranged tiny sandwiches and cakes.

Invite some friends or loved ones over to your place to enjoy this ritual with you. (If you don't own some of these items, borrow them or search local rummage sales or antique stores for inexpensive options.) Create and mail lovely paper invitations complete with your best sophisticated hand lettering. Brainstorm a menu that matches the tastes of the people coming or the season of the event, and offer two or three types of high-quality tea that you brew yourself. And be sure to hold out your pinkies, of course.

Give Yourself a Time Limit

Earth signs are known for being hard workers; they're resourceful and know just how to tackle tasks to make them manageable. They're also notoriously persistent when they're working to achieve their goals. Being productive and getting things done feels great to driven earth signs.

Stay on top of your to-do list with this productivity hack! Simply set a time limit with a timer to get your task done. Since you know you only have a limited time frame, you'll stay focused, quicken your pace, and accomplish a lot more than you expected. You'll feel satisfied and proud of all you'll be able to complete.

Reward Your Patience

———————————

In today's fast-paced world, it's important to stay patient, even when lines are slow, orders are misplaced, and Mercury in retrograde causes all kinds of confusion with communication. Luckily, earth signs are known for their ability to stay calm and forgiving. That's a great quality to maintain, so make sure you reward yourself on those days when your patience has been truly tested.

Whether it's enjoying a glass of fine wine, listening to some new music, or splurging on something you've had your eye on for a while, make sure to protect yourself from negativity and do something relaxing and restorative for you and you alone.

Spring for an Expensive Bottle of Wine

———————————

Life is too short to drink inexpensive wine *all* the time. Every once in a while, treat yourself to an expensive, high-quality bottle of wine. As an earth sign, you can appreciate the finer things in life, and you have a great sense of taste. Ask an employee at your local liquor store for a recommendation based on your preferences, or reach for a longtime favorite of yours.

Take out your nice glassware, let the bottle breathe, and then swirl and sip slowly so you can really taste the subtle notes in the glass as you relax and unwind.

Enjoy the Nutty Taste of Barley

Barley is an ancient whole grain full of fiber, protein, and vitamin B, and featuring an earthy, nutty taste. It offers an impressive array of health benefits: it can lower blood pressure, boost heart health, minimize inflammation, improve digestion, and control weight since it keeps you feeling full. Beyond this plethora of good reasons to eat it, barley is a perfect match for Virgo—after all, the Greeks represent Virgo as Persephone, goddess of the grain harvest!

Perhaps best of all, barley is easy to cook and incorporate into many meals. Add it to soups in place of rice or pasta. Toss it into green salads for a chewy boost in flavor and protein. You can even cook it on the stovetop to eat for breakfast like oatmeal. Search your favorite recipe websites or cookbooks for enticing barley recipes.

Dance It Off

You know it's important to take care of your body by exercising. But did you know that earth signs have a good sense of rhythm and may find a new workout routine through dancing? It's also a great way to add fun into an existing exercise schedule or try something new so your usual routine doesn't get boring.

Try a peaceful ballet class for discipline, or experiment with jazz and hip-hop for a fun, high-energy workout. Or look for other dance-inspired classes like Zumba or barre, which combine dance elements and workout styles for unique and challenging programs.

Train for a Marathon

———————

Patient earth signs are in it for the long haul; their workout style is more marathon than sprint. These slow and steady athletes are disciplined and committed to achieving their goals.

Your body will thank you for taking on activities like running, biking, dancing, or even jump roping! You may even want to train to run a marathon, or participate in a triathlon, which will really test your endurance with a series of swimming, biking, and running challenges. These activities will keep you feeling refreshed and rejuvenated, while helping you develop strength and stamina.

Try a Stress-Free Workout

If the thought of running a marathon has you sweating already, don't worry! There are other workouts perfect for earth signs, like learning to work on a balance bar or taking some beginners' gymnastics skills classes. With your disciplined attitude, you'll be able to focus on improving your strength and stability while mastering these challenging skills.

These workouts can be a great way to take care of your body and keep it healthy and toned. But they can also be a much-needed opportunity to relax and compose yourself on an otherwise busy day. The focus you'll need to master carefully controlled movements will help take your mind off the stress of your day and give you a chance to recharge.

Look Before You Leap

Earth signs are logical thinkers, who often like to fully evaluate their options before making a decision. They're seeking safety and security, so they aren't interested in taking big risks. Taking that essential time to think things through can be a major benefit for their mental health. You certainly don't want to be rushed into making a decision!

If you find yourself faced with a problem or challenging situation, think it over privately before confiding in a friend. Give yourself permission to reclaim the time and space you need for yourself. You'll feel more confident sharing your decisions and more comfortable moving forward.

Go Forest Bathing

Just like regular bathing involves immersing yourself in water, forest bathing is the process of immersing yourself in trees and nature. The Environmental Protection Agency recently found that the average American spends 93 percent of their time indoors, but earth signs especially benefit from regular contact with Mother Earth.

Forest bathing is an easy, relaxing way to enjoy the outdoors. Silence your devices so you savor your senses—see the various shades of green, smell the various flowers, feel the crisp air, and listen to the crunch of branches under your feet.

Finish a Meal with Peppermint Tea

Virgo often needs a little extra help ensuring smooth digestion. One easy idea is to drink a cup of bright peppermint tea after your meal.

Peppermint tea is known to help digestion while minimizing any gas or bloating. You can buy peppermint tea at the store, or make your own at home. To make your own, simply buy fresh peppermint (choose organic, if possible), clean it, and then crush the leaves with a mortar and pestle (or the back of a spoon). Place the crushed leaves into a mug (put them in a tea infuser or tea ball if you have one) and add boiling water. Let steep for 7–12 minutes to desired flavor intensity, and then strain the leaves out (if applicable) before drinking.

Declutter Your Home and Your Mind

E arth signs are known to hang onto too many belongings. While you may enjoy the memories that these items bring, keeping too many of them will eventually clutter your physical and mental space.

Take a day to go through your possessions and decide what's most meaningful to you. If an item has outlasted its usefulness to you, donate it to someone who would enjoy it more. When you've finished, take notice of the physical space you've created and meditate in or near it for a few minutes if possible. You'll likely find that you've also freed up mental space for new ideas.

Get Crafty

Virgo has many creative talents. If you haven't tried sewing yet, you might find it to be a peaceful, relaxing hobby—and a great way to express yourself artistically.

It might seem intimidating, but there are actually lots of easy sewing patterns that beginners can make. From shift dresses and boxer shorts to tote bags and pillowcases, you can find patterns and fabrics to fit your style and personality. Look for a used or hand-me-down sewing machine and read the instructions, or take a beginners' class to learn the basics. Then set up your own sewing basket with your equipment (such as needles, thimbles, high-quality scissors, and pins) and start stitching!

Press Wildflowers

The simplicity and whimsy of pressed flowers can mesh well with many types of home décor. On your next trip outside, look for wildflowers that you can bring home, set between two sheets of wax paper, and store inside a large, heavy book for a week. Then carefully slide the flowers into a prepared frame that compliments their color and style.

One wildflower that might speak to Virgo is Queen Anne's lace. It is said to represent sanctuary, and has an interesting legend behind it: Queen Anne, wife of King James I of England, was trying to sew lace in a pattern as beautiful as a flower. In so doing, she pricked her finger. Her blood is said to be the purple-red center seen on some Queen Anne's lace flowers.

Get a Pet Cat

Virgo loves pets, especially cats. These intelligent and low-maintenance pets offer friendship and can help you relax, recenter, and slow down for a while. If you don't have a cat at home, visit a local shelter to meet some potential pets and decide which breed might be right for you. Whether it's a lovable tabby or a regal Siamese, cats can add a wonderful dimension to your life.

If you already have a furry feline friend, be sure to make lots of quality time to spend together...and consider getting another one!

Protect Your Throat

———

Earth signs are connected to several parts of the body including the throat. Communication is key to earth signs, and when something interferes with that communication, whether it be a blocked throat chakra or even a sore throat, earth signs' confidence and strength can suffer. So protect your throat! In the colder months wear a scarf or muffler around your throat. Try meditating with turquoise to open up your throat chakra. If you do get a sore throat, treat it quickly and naturally with a saltwater gargle, honey, lemon water, or ginger tea.

Color Your Home
Like the Earth

Earth signs tend to feel most at ease in their homes when they are surrounded by calming earth tones. Greens, browns, and whites are great choices to decorate your home. Of course, given your simple tastes, you'll want to make sure these colors are muted versions, nothing too garish or bright. Loud colors will actually take away from your comfort level at home, something you don't want to do. Also wood floors, dark finishes, and plain walls will all add to the elegance and polished feeling of your home while fitting in perfectly with your classic and understated vibe.

Embrace Your Practicality

———————————

Sometimes earth signs get a bad reputation for their serious sides, but your practicality is really a positive thing. Earth signs are incredibly sensible and resourceful, and they have a talent for solving problems that others give up on. You come up with real-world solutions that actually work! You love to ponder and thoroughly understand a problem or concept, and like to make charts, graphs, or diagrams to further explore the topic. You stick with a problem through the long haul and come up with a solution that works—celebrate the positives of being the perfect problem-solver!

Try to Compromise

_____

Earth signs have so many wonderful qualities, but one characteristic that might trouble you sometimes is your stubbornness. Instead of getting down on yourself, turn that trait around by consciously working to compromise whenever possible.

For example, if a friend wants to go out to one type of restaurant and you want another, talk for a few minutes to determine someplace you'd both like. If your partner prefers one couch but you want to buy another, work out a solution based on what's best for your space. These types of thoughtful, caring conversations go a long way toward ensuring harmony in your relationships.

Organize Yourself with an Apothecary or Filing Cabinet

Virgo loves containers of all shapes and sizes, and for all sorts of uses. One useful storage spot for your house might be a Chinese apothecary cabinet, which features many drawers to keep everything in its place. It's perfect for storing small items like keys or brushes that can otherwise clutter busy spots in your house.

For your paper-based storage, look for a sturdy file cabinet. You can organize your documents with tabbed folders for easy access. And don't worry, file cabinets aren't only offered in heavy, gray metal anymore—you can find lots of visually interesting file cabinets online.

Take In a Ballet

Ballet isn't just for little kids in pastel outfits—adult ballet performances are a stunning show of physical beauty and skill mastery, accompanied by breathtaking music. As a Virgo you can appreciate these accomplishments, along with the intricate costumes and spellbinding stories.

Check your local area for visiting professional ballet troupes, or watch a local college or dance school's top ballet group.

Whether you watch a classic favorite, like *Swan Lake* or *Giselle*, or a newer dance production, like *Maple Leaf Rag*, you'll no doubt sit in awe of the dancers' strength, grace, and poise, and come away with a newfound appreciation for this elegant expression of movement.

Try the Extended Locust Pose

Practicing yoga is a wonderful way to build strength while calming your mind. For Virgo, poses that encourage good digestion are especially applicable.

One such pose is the Extended Locust Pose. It will strengthen your back and abdominal muscles, improve your posture, and massage your digestive tract. This is not a beginner's pose, so make sure to practice this with your yoga instructor for technique guidance.

To do Extended Locust Pose, lie on your belly on a yoga mat, extending your arms out in front of you. Inhale, then lift your arms, head, and legs off the mat toward the ceiling. Hold for five breaths, and then release back to the mat and rest. Try doing this pose 30 minutes after eating a large meal.

See the Big Picture

Virgo is a very detail-oriented person, which is a big plus in many areas of life. Yet, even as you keep track of the little things, be sure to take a step back periodically to see the big picture as well.

As you unwind every night, try to push the little annoyances of your day out of your head and, instead, remind yourself of all that you have to be grateful for. Whether it's your good health, great friends, supportive family, rewarding career, or even simpler things like a roof over your head and food to eat, you undoubtedly have things in your life that make you feel blessed. Make sure to recognize them daily.

Put Clean White Sheets on Your Bed

Is there anything more inviting than a comfy bed that's just been freshly made with crisp white sheets? If your sheets are getting faded and threadbare, it's time to invest in new ones to ensure a restful night's sleep.

As you put the new sheets on the bed, be sure to tuck everything in very tightly—Virgo likes to feel secure in her bed. Make sure your nightstand contains only what you need to get through your night, like a book and some tissues. You might also consider spraying a relaxing essential oil like vanilla (diluted according to instructions) onto your sheets before you go to sleep at night.

Keep Things Slow and Steady

———————

E arth signs know that nothing great ever comes easily or quickly. In fact, their combined patience and discipline is one of their most admirable traits and allows them to stick things out for the long run. Earth signs like to meticulously plan and *hate* to rush. Actually, rushing through a task will cause you stress and may lead to mistakes (something you don't tolerate well). Whether working or playing, you should take a slow and steady approach, and your final results will be better quality and more long-lasting than those of the hurried competition. Keep a steady pace when at home and at work and you'll produce your best results.

Recite Affirmations

Affirmations are short, powerful, positive phrases that you can recite aloud or silently to yourself to help bring about positive change in your life. They're easy to remember and simple to work into your day—you can recite them while you practice yoga, while you take a shower, or while on your morning commute.

Virgo is by nature analytical and hardworking. An affirmation like "I effortlessly make order in my world" speaks to where Virgo's strengths lie and how keeping order feels like an easy task to her, not a daunting struggle. Repeating these words can help you feel confident, empowered, and energized.

Relax with a Spa Day

Finding time to relax with friends can be a challenge with everyone's busy schedules. But merging a get-together with some soothing self-care and pampering might just suddenly clear everyone's calendar!

Virgo loves to help others, and organizing a group trip to the spa is a wonderful way to show others that you care about their well-being. Check in with people's preferences—massages, nails, facials—and organize a schedule with the spa. If the venue allows, bring some seltzer water and small snacks for people to nibble on between appointments. You'll all leave the spa grateful for the good company and the feeling of tranquility in your bodies.

Plant Some Perennials

There's something so reassuring about the first flowers of spring. Prepare your garden for a riot of spring color by planting bulbs in the fall.

While it may seem like nothing is happening over the course of the winter and early spring, magic is taking place beneath the soil. When the snow has melted, you'll start to see green sprouts—your plants are growing! You've created your own miniharvest (perfect since Virgo is the symbol of the harvest) of colorful blooms. You can consider tender purple crocuses, bright yellow daffodils, or bold red tulips. These flowers when cut will brighten your home and your heart.

Embrace Imperfection

Virgo is hardworking and wants everything to be perfect. And that goal is admirable—but also unattainable.

Instead, learn to love imperfection. Sometimes, you can teach yourself this by looking at a situation that seems imperfect from a different perspective. For example, if there are parts of your body that you aren't thrilled with, switch that thought and instead remind yourself of the *astounding* number of amazing things your body does for you every single day. Or, if you're unhappy with a decision you've made, think of it as learning a life lesson. And just as a baby learning to walk will fall dozens of times, so too will you "fall" as you learn things. And just as you wouldn't judge a baby for those spills, neither should you think harshly of yourself for yours. Love all the parts of yourself, imperfections and all.

Schedule Therapy Sessions

While bottling everything up inside might get you through a rough patch, it's not a long-term strategy for sound mental health. If you haven't already, consider talking to a therapist to unload and work through difficult situations.

Virgo tends to hold in her mental processes, which can backfire later when they build up and become overwhelming. Find a therapist whose expertise matches your needs, and share your life concerns. No problem is too big or too small for a therapist to help with, so don't let that fear hold you back. Asking for help is a brave, mature, and healthy thing to do—so show your mind the same type of self-care you show your body at the gym and talk through your problems.

Paint a Rock

Earth signs like to be crafty, so let your creativity shine by painting a symbol of the earth—a rock! Head outdoors to find a few suitable rocks—usually, flat, smooth ones are the easiest canvas. You might want to start by painting a base layer of white paint so other colors show up better. Add details or hand lettering with fine-tip permanent markers.

Let the experience be quiet and meditative—listen to ambient music as you paint. When your design is complete, cover it with a clear coat of Mod Podge (following the directions) to seal it in. You can keep the rock for yourself as a reminder of your connection to the earth, or pass along its good energy and give it as a gift to a friend or loved one.

Set a New Goal for Yourself

Many people use the start of a new year to set goals. But there's no need to wait for January 1 to do that. As an earth sign, you'll benefit from setting a practical goal for yourself, and then tracking your progress, no matter what time of year it is. Whether you're trying to get rid of a bad habit or institute a healthy new one, setting a goal and noting check-points along the way makes you much more likely to be successful.

When you think of a goal, write it down and post it in a place where you'll see it frequently. Be sure to reward yourself every time you meet one of your checkpoints to keep yourself motivated.

Add Fennel to Your Diet

———————

Fennel is a strong-smelling herb known for its abilities to soothe the intestines and digestive system. Stomachaches can be a problem for Virgo, but this herb can be a lifesaver.

You can chop raw fennel bulb into soups, salads, or vegetable dishes; use the feathery fennel fronds (the green tops) as an unexpected salad topper; or roast fennel bulbs for a tender texture. Fennel contains a lot of vitamin C, fiber, iron, and potassium, so fennel isn't just good for your stomach!

Choose Only the Softest Fabrics

Earth signs have a highly developed sense of touch, so choose soft materials for your clothes and sheets. Don't spend your day feeling distracted by an itchy wool sweater or spend all night tossing and turning on scratchy sheets. Restore your healthy skin (and cheerful attitude!) by choosing materials like cashmere, silk, organic cotton, and suede.

You'll prefer any materials or fabrics that touch your skin to be soft and comforting, so go ahead and splurge on high thread count sheets, fluffy towels, and warm, downy blankets.

Relax with Lavender Spray

After a long day at work, coupled with regular home and family responsibilities, it can be difficult to quiet your mind. Reconnecting with the earth through a floral essence spray might be just the ticket.

Lavender is well known for its soothing, calming properties. Though you can use a lavender-scented candle, a diluted essential oil spray can be even more effective. Simply add some drops of lavender essential oil (diluted according to instructions) to a small spray bottle. Spritz it on your couch or pillow and proceed with your usual routine. The aromatherapy will work its magic as you go about your business.

Treat Your Sweet Tooth

E arth signs are known for their appreciation for the finer things and may enjoy opportunities to indulge. You might find you instinctually gravitate toward sweet flavors over anything savory. While it's certainly important to eat a balanced diet and enjoy everything in moderation, a sweet treat or two can be just the pick-me-up you need to improve a grumpy mood or curb an unhealthier craving.

Although you may prefer to stick with your reliable, tried-and-true favorites, prevent yourself from becoming "stuck" by looking for your sweet fix in unexpected places. Expand your cultural palate by trying food from different cuisines.

Take Up Chess

If you're trying to spend less time in front of screens, you should consider some traditional methods of entertainment—like board games!

Chess, in particular, is a good fit for the analytical Virgo mind. Plus, you can play with a friend and enjoy some quiet social downtime as well. If you have never played, watch an online tutorial or read a book about chess strategy before you start a game. Then ask a friend to join you for a friendly match. Before long you'll find yourself looking forward to the precision of setting up the board and the intellectual challenge of making your moves.

Send Flowers...to Yourself!

No matter the season, earth signs benefit from having plants around. Just like you need plants in your home, you also need some for your office. Especially during dreary rainy days or cold months, you'll need something to reframe your mind-set and spark a positive attitude throughout the day.

Try a monthly flower or plant subscription service to get your plant pick-me-up. Whatever your preference, treat yourself to the perfect desk accessory, with options ranging from handcrafted bouquets to potted plants...or even a succulent or two! No secret admirer is needed—these services will deliver plants of your choice to your desk all year round.

Listen to Your Body

Virgo is generally in tune with her body—
sometimes almost *too* much, fearing that
something's wrong all the time. But that inward
connection is a powerful gift, so treasure it!

Your body is always communicating with you—
whether alerting you to basic needs like hunger and
fatigue, or mental stresses like feeling overwhelmed
or stressed out. When you hear these messages, be
sure to address them promptly. Ignoring your body's
needs is a surefire way to get run-down, exhausted, or
burnt-out. But, unfortunately, many of us do this from
time to time thanks to work or other commitments.

So, whether it's leaving your work desk to eat a
healthy lunch slowly, or going to bed early instead of
bingeing that show, make sure to give your body what
it needs.

Create a Room of Comfort

Everyone needs a space, even if it is just one room in your house or apartment, where you can just get away and relax in comfort. Comfortable surroundings are important for earth signs in particular; not only do they crave them, but they also feel the most at peace there.

So make sure at least one room in your home is filled with plush, cushy furniture. Big pieces of furniture are important for comfort, too, because they give you a sense of security and a feeling that you are staying put. Overstuffed pillows and soft blankets would make nice accents here as well. Create a room that makes you feel safe and snug, a place you can go to find relaxation and peace and forget the stresses of your life, and you will be a truly happy earth sign.

Add a Soundtrack
to Your Daily Chores

———————————

S ometimes, chores get to be boring and stressful for even the most practical and grounded of earth signs. And whether it's breaking out the vacuum cleaner or dusting every horizontal surface in your home, everyone has that one task that seems so unpleasant and difficult to finish.

For earth signs this is the perfect time to turn to your love of music to keep yourself mentally alert and refocus yourself on the task at hand. Whistling while completing your everyday tasks will keep you relaxed and help you tackle even your least favorite chores with ease.

Go for the Goal!

I f you're looking for a team sport, keep in mind the earth signs' tendencies to look for ways to use their strength and stamina. Try sports like soccer or volleyball that combine those skills. With team sports like these, you'll be able to take care of your body and develop strong, supportive friendships, all while having the added benefit of keeping your feet in your comfort zone...firmly on the ground.

Your endurance will keep you going from the beginning of the game to the very last second. And your goal-oriented nature is sure to keep you on the winning team as you help your team toward victory!

Treat Yourself to Chocolate

E arth signs love chocolate, and it's a wonderful way to treat yourself. Some earth signs may have trouble with dairy though, so try a good-quality rich dark chocolate to indulge in. Not only does dark chocolate taste heavenly, but it benefits your health too. Dark chocolate helps lower blood pressure, is a powerful source of antioxidants, and reduces your heart disease risk. Eat your dark chocolate straight—or melt some in a double boiler, pour into a silicone mold ice cube tray, sprinkle on some healthy nuts and dried fruits, and allow to set for a mouthwatering treat you can feel good about.

Meditate in Nature

I t's important to take a few moments to yourself to relax, refresh, and gather your thoughts. To get some peace of mind, try meditating in nature. Particularly for thoughtful earth signs, this time-out ritual can be helpful to clear your mind.

One option is to find a comfortable seated position, close your eyes, and focus on your breathing and the present moment before allowing yourself to pay attention to the natural world around you. Or try meditating while walking and see how nature interacts with each of your senses. What sounds can you hear? What are you able to touch? How does your body feel? Earth signs may find it particularly helpful to meditate on the flowers and trees around them.

Prepare Meals Ahead of Time

Virgo loves to plan, so be sure to extend that skill to your meal planning as well. Instead of leaving the decision 'til the last minute, try spending some time on the weekend (or whatever time you have free) figuring out what you'll eat and when.

Meal planning like this is beneficial in so many ways. First, it makes your grocery shopping much easier and more focused because you'll know what ingredients you need to buy and can get them all at once, instead of stopping multiple times throughout the week. Second, you're more likely to try new recipes or foods because you can check out recipes ahead of time. Third, you can even start to prep certain ingredients on the weekends (for example, chopping carrots for a soup you'll make on Tuesday) or use timesavers like slow cookers to ease the pressure on weeknights. The time and headaches you'll save will leave you free for unwinding and relaxing.

Keep a Health Journal

Part of practicing good self-care is paying attention to trends and observations about how you feel physically and mentally. Luckily, Virgo loves statistics and data—so give in to your system-loving side and keep a journal of how you are feeling.

You can decide how to keep your records. Think about what aspects of your health you'd like to focus on—it might be blood pressure, heart rate, weight, stress levels, digestion—and then create a goal around that concern. In your journal, divide the space into columns or sections where you can track information, whether in number or written form. Periodically, go back over your notes so you can find patterns or celebrate your progress.

Help Out an Animal Charity

Helping others is a Virgo trademark and it's also a great way to take care of yourself too. Spending time lending a hand to those less fortunate will help fulfill you spiritually and make you feel like you're making real change in the world.

Virgo in particular might feel a strong connection to organizations that help animals. Whether it's protecting a habitat, engaging with the animals, or raising awareness, you can lend a hand to creatures great and small. Think about what skills you can offer—maybe your record keeping and detail-oriented nature?—and brainstorm the most effective way to help that chosen particular group. As you see the fruits of your labor paying off for the organization, you'll no doubt feel proud, happy, and motivated to keep helping.

Wrap Yourself in Warmth

There is something so special and nurturing about being wrapped in something cuddly. Earth signs especially like to feel warm, protected, and comfortable. A good way to accomplish this feeling in your home is to find a thick, warm comforter for your bed. Bonus points if you can make one yourself, maybe even stitching in some pieces of a childhood blankie. Not a crafty person? There is no shortage of ultra-plush comforters available to buy online. Try to get one in a deep, rich earth tone to compliment your earth sign! Want to kick the comfort up a notch? Try warming your sheets in the dryer right before you get into bed!

Visit a Local Museum

Many of us only think of going to museums when we're visiting a new city or a special exhibit is in town. But these local cultural centers (often right in our own neighborhoods!) are incredible resources for expanding your intellectual horizons.

Virgo loves learning new things, and museums are excellent teachers. Taking care of your brain is just as important as taking care of your body, and teaching your brain new things is a great way to stay mentally fit. You can read about the artist who painted a masterpiece at an art museum, learn about nanotechnology through hands-on activities at a science museum, or soak in the history of an area by looking at artifacts at a local heritage museum. Think about a subject that interests you and find a fascinating museum to explore.

Play Number Puzzles

——————————

Number puzzles help keep your mind sharp, just like crossword puzzles. Virgo often likes the exactness of numbers, so these activities are the perfect option for your logical mind.

You can find sudoku or other number puzzles in book format, through apps, or online. Instead of mindlessly scrolling through your social media feeds on your train ride to work, try these puzzles. Or fill in a few at your lunch break or while you're in the waiting room before a doctor's appointment. Your brain will appreciate the stimulation, and you'll likely find yourself progressing from beginner puzzles to expert level in no time.

Help a Friend with a Problem

Watching a friend go through a tough time can be a painful experience. One way to support is to offer them help or advice, if your friend is open to it.

As a Virgo you are very good at looking at problems and thinking of possible solutions. Your objective insights and potential answers might make a significant difference to your friend. Just remember to be sensitive to the big picture; don't push too hard, and, above all, listen and be compassionate. You'll show yourself to be reliable, thoughtful, and caring—traits that are valuable to your friend and can make you proud of yourself too.

Go Meatless (Sometimes)

You've probably heard that you should keep an eye on your meat intake. But does that mean you have to give up hamburgers forever? No. Instead, adopt a "flexitarian" ("flexible vegetarian") diet, devised by dietitian Dawn Jackson Blatner, and just go meatless periodically.

Flexitarians want to eat more plant-based food on a regular basis, but also want the flexibility of eating meat once in a while. Your body—especially your digestive system—will be healthier when your diet consists of a higher percentage of plant-based foods.

Virgo needs to take good care of her often troublesome digestive system—and Virgo's symbol is that of a harvest—so this plant-focused diet is a good match for you.

Try Aromatherapy

E arth signs are closely in touch with all of their senses. Aromatherapy is a simple and easy way for you to connect with and savor your sense of smell. You can enjoy a citrus body wash to energize yourself during your morning shower, sip some ginger tea to recharge in a midafternoon slump, read in a room scented by a soothing vanilla candle, or spritz (diluted according to instructions) lavender essential oil on your pillow before bed to relax.

When you begin practicing aromatherapy regularly, you'll find yourself more in tune with your sense of smell all the time. You'll notice the scent of your neighbor's flowers, the mixture of flavors wafting from your favorite restaurant, and the earthy smells after a spring rain.

Treat Yourself to
New Loungewear

Everyone owns some favorite sweats or comfy shirts. But many of us wear this loungewear until it's ripped, stretched out, and stained. Take stock of what you currently own and see if some of it can be recycled or donated. Then treat yourself to some new items, and enjoy them the next time you're unwinding at home after a long day in less-than-comfortable work clothes.

Earth signs love to be comfortable, so repeat this process once a year. You'll look forward to relaxing and recharging in your new pieces!

Visit a Farmers' Market

Farmers' markets offer an astounding array of local produce and homemade foods. You might be surprised at what's being grown right around you. There's sure to be a market in your area—find out its schedule and pop in regularly. Let your senses savor the offerings—see the brightly colored displays, smell the fresh peaches and herbs, and maybe snag a sample bite that a stall is offering. Look for organic produce, which is good for the environment and your health.

Try to find recipes that use your farmers' market haul for a couple of dinners a week, and grab the whole fruits for easy snacks on the go.

Invest Your Money

———————

Earth signs are conscientious—money matters tend to come easy for you. Still, you want to be sure that your money isn't just sitting in an account somewhere. Put it to work for you by making wise investments.

Do some research with trusted sources to be sure your investments are smart, and work with a broker or on your own to make the actual transactions. Check in periodically to see how your accounts are doing and make adjustments as needed. Over time, your investments will grow and you'll enjoy even more fortune.

Let Go of Old Hurts

If you've ever endured an embarrassing situation or difficult interaction with someone, you've probably also replayed it again and again in your mind: wishing you did something differently, wishing it didn't happen at all. Ruminating like this on the interaction isn't serving you well, though. In fact, the best thing you can do is learn from it and then let it go.

Virgo in particular can replay these situations far longer than is necessary. One way to move on is to close your eyes and visualize the situation tied to you with dozens of strings. Breathe deeply, and imagine yourself cutting the strings one by one, and letting the situation gently float away forever. This exercise can help you free your mind of these mental blocks so you're not weighed down by them.

Sign Up for a POUND Class

If you haven't heard of a POUND class, Virgo, it's about time you give it a try. This drum-based exercise is a great workout, plus it's fun! If you don't think you have rhythm, think again. After all, Virgo is great at counting, and finding the beat in a POUND class is based on counting (think *five, six, seven, eight*!).

Whether you've played the drums in the past or have never played an instrument in your life, you're sure to find a local POUND class that fits your schedule and your pace. Bring a friend along with you, or just get ready to meet new people. Either way, you'll probably leave class tired but laughing and feeling uplifted.

Indulge in the Warmth of Cinnamon

Nothing conjures up feelings of warmth like the smell of cinnamon. It brings back memories of warm, comforting foods on cool, crisp fall days. But cinnamon is not just for autumn time; in fact, it is perfect for earth signs to use all year round. When you're cooking, choose warm spices like cinnamon over sharp and peppery spices, as these tend not to agree with an earth sign's delicate palate. As an added bonus, cinnamon is good for your heart health, helps regulate your blood sugar, boosts your brain function, and offers your body protection from diabetes.

Cinnamon is a marvelous addition to both sweet and savory meals and will add the hint of spice you crave without the burning aftereffects of other spices. Add cinnamon to your favorite foods including oatmeal, pancakes, yogurt, peanut or almond butter, chilies and soups, and even your coffee!

Daydream to Calm Your Mind

In today's world it's easy to have your brain running nonstop. Work, family, and other responsibilities are on your mind—you probably jump from one practical thought to the next with no break. It's time to change that and give your head a break!

Allow yourself time to daydream about something positive every day—whether it's while you shower in the morning, during your lunch break, or before you go to bed. Banish thoughts of bills or deadlines and think of something wonderful—a favorite vacation spot, a warm memory with a loved one, or a life goal you're trying to achieve. You'll find this practice leaves you mentally energized, refreshed, and balanced.

Keep a Bullet Journal

Ryder Carroll, a digital product designer, came up with the simple yet revolutionary idea of bullet journaling, or BuJo for short. Instead of logging long, cumbersome journal or calendar entries, just jot down bulleted lists. You can customize the bullets and lists how you want, but the key is that the process shouldn't be overwhelming. Writing in the journal is actually an act of mindfulness that helps you organize your thoughts quickly and easily.

Check out www.bulletjournal.com and see how easy the process can be. Journaling in this simple way will help you empty your mind of the responsibilities swirling around it so you can keep track of everything in an organized way that works for you.

Plan a Spring Bloom Trip

Spring flowers are a sign of rebirth and new beginnings. Taking time to enjoy them is a powerful way of re-centering yourself and enjoying the beauty of nature.

You can look at spring blooms wherever you live, or take a trip somewhere instead—maybe to see the bold colors of tulips in the Netherlands; the inimitable cherry blossoms in Japan or Washington, DC; the millions of cheerful daffodils in Gibbs Gardens in Georgia; or the Portland Rose Festival in Oregon. No matter what type of flower you enjoy, savoring them en masse is a humbling and relaxing experience.

Quiet Your Inner Critic

We all struggle sometimes with that little voice inside our heads that makes us doubt ourselves. Are we smart enough, fit enough, productive enough, wealthy enough? Virgo is naturally a critical thinker, which is a useful skill if you're analyzing a business proposal, but is detrimental when it's turned inward on yourself.

If you have the tendency to criticize yourself, try to stop those thoughts and turn them around. Instead of telling yourself you're not healthy enough, remind yourself of all the smart food and exercise choices you make. Instead of wondering why you're not further ahead in your career, think of all your many accomplishments. Reframing your situation like this is a powerful way to quiet your inner critic and celebrate all that you are.

Create Your Own Pottery

———————

You've probably seen gorgeous pottery in stores, but have you ever tried to make it yourself? For a fun activity, work with some clay to make your own creation, be it a simple bowl, a mug for your morning coffee, or a decoration to give as a gift. Earth signs are in touch with their senses, and this hands-on craft allows you to get your hands dirty and really savor your sense of touch.

Take a class at a local art center or craft store where you can make a piece from start to finish. Once you've made your creation, you can have it fired by the professionals in its natural color or painted.

Make Your Home Your Haven

E arth signs like to feel protected in their home, almost as if it were a sheltered cave. A feeling of enclosure may seem stifling to other signs, but for earth signs there is a comfort in the closeness and warmth. Emphasize that feeling in your home by decorating with darker colors and with accents such as lamps with shades to give off a soft glow in your rooms. This warm and welcoming shelter will make you feel protected and safe whenever you enter it.

Whip Up a Delicious Green Smoothie

F eeling tired, hungry, and de-energized during a late afternoon slump? Instead of overindulging in an unhealthy snack you eat mindlessly, restore yourself with a smoothie made with fresh, leafy greens from the earth. Kale, arugula, and spinach are good sources of folate, fiber, and vitamins A and C, plus they are filled with antioxidants and are known to improve heart health.

Grab one at a juice bar near you, or make your own, adding chunks of pear, honey, or apple to the greens to create a bit of sweetness in your drink. Savor each sip, and notice how it makes you feel restored and rejuvenated with no guilt!

Make Time to Read Books

_____

It can be difficult to fit books into your busy schedule. One easy way to find time is to swap some TV-watching time for reading time, even if it's just a couple of hours a week. Virgo is ruled by Mercury, who is the messenger god and ruler of the written word, so reading books is a particularly effective self-care practice for you.

If you're having trouble deciding what to read, look to fellow Virgo authors, like Leo Tolstoy, Stephen King, Agatha Christie, Mary Shelley, or D.H. Lawrence. You might find that their characters and plotlines are especially interesting to you. Whether you pop into a bookstore to grab a hard copy or download the ebook on an app on your smartphone, you'll find this pastime relaxing and intellectually stimulating.

Splurge Once in a While

———————————

Virgo is very organized and stays on budget, which is a skill you should celebrate! But every now and again, allow yourself to splurge on something you don't necessarily need, but would like to have.

Ask yourself what would make you happy—whether it is a new pair of shoes, a fancy watch, or a cool cordless speaker—and get it! And don't worry, you don't need to bust your budget completely. Just the act of treating yourself will make you feel joyful, especially if it's a treat you've been wanting for some time.

Talk to a Friend

These days we often rely on texting to keep in touch with friends. While that's a good method a lot of the time, it's also vital to keep friendships strong by talking on the phone or, even better, in person. Earth signs are very loyal, and your friends are important to you. Show them that by prioritizing them in your schedule. Find time to catch up so you can move past emojis and nurture the type of close bond you and your friend deserve.

If finding a mutually agreeable time is proving difficult, get creative—for example, take a walk or jog together so you can exercise *and* catch up.

Enjoy an Herbal Foot Soak

After a long day you need to get off your feet and relax. An herbal foot soak is an excellent way for Virgo to reconnect with the harvest while restoring her aching arches, moisturizing dry heels, and improving circulation.

You can purchase a premixed herbal infusion foot soak. Or you can create your own herbal combinations using 2 cups of Epsom salts as your base mixed with an essential oil (diluted first according to instructions) appropriate for bath soaks. Use ¼ cup of your Epsom salt/diluted herb mixture in a basin of warm water and soak your tired feet for 15 minutes.

Or, if you don't have that much time to spare, rub moisturizer (creams containing lavender and aloe vera among their ingredients are a soothing and calming option) on your weary feet.

Take One Step at a Time

—————

Some people like to jump headfirst into a problem and work it out while trapped in the midst of it. Well that may be great for them, but the thought of it gives earth signs nervous feelings. Earth signs approach almost everything they do with a methodical, step-by-step approach. This method allows you to thoroughly understand exactly what you're getting yourself into, come up with a well-thought-out plan to solve it, and then actually resolve the issue. While it may take you a little more prep time than other people when faced with a problem, you often have a higher success rate too. Breaking down obstacles into clear steps makes earth signs the best problem-solvers around.

Do the Wind-Relieving Yoga Pose

Since Virgo rules the intestines, you might sometimes have trouble with gas, bloating, and indigestion. This yoga pose can work wonders on these issues (while strengthening your back and abdominal muscles), and it's simple to do.

Lie down on your back on a yoga mat. Bring one knee up toward your chest, holding your leg steady with both hands, and then lift your head forward toward your knee. Hold the pose for a few breaths, release your leg, and then switch legs. Do this as often as necessary, after meals or before bedtime.

Keep an Eye on Your Body Language

———————————

Some scientists believe that more than half of human communication is nonverbal—meaning, it's conveyed by body language. That means that facial expressions, hand gestures, and posture tell people a lot about how you feel. Because Virgo can often live in her head, her body language might show her to be cold, while she's actually just reserved and shy.

Try to be alert to this potential misconception and be mindful of your posture and facial expressions, especially when you meet new people. You are actually warm and caring, so let people see that side of you too. If it feels right, you can smile and offer a friendly handshake.

Add More Fiber to Your Diet

Taking care of your digestive system is important work for Virgo. Fiber is a crucial part of healthy digestion, and you probably already know a few whole-grain sources, such as oatmeal and barley. But did you also know you can get fiber from lots of other types of foods, such as split peas, black beans, artichokes, Brussels sprouts, raspberries, and blackberries?

Most adults need 25–38 grams of fiber a day, so keep that number in the back of your head as you plan your meals. Throw a few raspberries on your lunch salad, add black beans to your taco, or whip up a split pea soup in your blender to add fiber to your diet in an easy and delicious way!

Build Endurance with Your Workouts

E xercise is proven to be one of the best forms of self-care you can do for your body and mind. But what if you are new to working out or just feel like it isn't your thing? Fortunately for you as an earth sign, the slow and steady approach also relates to how you should be working out. Earth signs are disciplined, dependable, and committed. So, when they exercise, they should choose workouts that require patience, precision, and a set routine.

Workouts that work your muscles at a slower pace will build your endurance and muscle strength without making you feel like your regime is hectic and out of your control. Training for races that require precision and problem-solving like a Tough Mudder, which is more about endurance than speed, is also a hit with earth signs.

Stick with the Classics

Treat yourself to a little shopping trip, but rather than buying the latest fad, shop for your sign. Style magazines and experts may tell you what's all the rage in fashion, but as an earth sign, you won't necessarily feel comfortable or strong—both things earth signs need in their lives—with what is trendy. Earth signs are all about the simple yet elegant look when it comes to fashion, as well as décor. You like things that are classic, well made, neat, and polished—think Audrey Hepburn (who is also an earth sign!) and George Clooney.

In terms of clothing, you feel more comfortable in the elegant and sophisticated and stay clear of the flashy, too tight, or too revealing. You value comfort, but that doesn't mean you don't look suave or glamorous; you like to make a statement without seeming like you are making a statement. So stick with the classics and you'll always exude an understated elegance.

Cook Dinner for Someone

————————

Getting together with friends and loved ones is one of the best ways to relax and truly be yourself. Virgo might enjoy cooking someone else dinner, because she likes to do things for other people.

Whether it's a romantic candlelit dinner for two, or a quiet meal with a longtime friend, you can extend the invitation, plan the meal, and then send your guest home with leftovers for the next day's lunch. The good company and the homemade food will leave you physically satisfied and mentally fulfilled.

Write in a Dream Journal

Ever had an interesting dream that you forgot the next morning? Since Virgo loves to analyze everything, keep a dream journal so you never forget your dreams again.

Leave a notebook and pencil by your bed, and quickly jot down a few keywords whenever you have a dream. In the morning review your notes and see if they help trigger a memory of your dream. Then search online or in a dream dictionary to see what the main parts might represent. Take a look at how color in your dreams can be interpreted by reading Dr. Betty L. Thompson's fascinating book *By the Light of Your Dreams* (available on www.bythelightofyourdreams.com). You could just learn something new about yourself or see a situation you're facing in a different light.

Whip Up a Detox Drink

We all overindulge from time to time, whether in sugar, alcohol, or other empty calories. After you've overdone it, you would benefit from a wholesome cleansing drink to help your body detox and right itself.

One all-natural drink that's easy to make is to combine 3 medium peeled sugar beets (including greens, trimmed), 1 medium carrot (peeled and trimmed), and ½ pound black seedless grapes (destemmed) in a blender. These fruits and veggies benefit the liver, which eliminates toxins, filters the blood, metabolizes nutrients, and performs many other functions. A simple drink like this can get you back on track with your usual healthy diet and restore your physical well-being.

Indulge in a Day Off

Earth signs are very practical and dependable, but they can take that dedication too far and end up overworking themselves. Treat yourself to days off from work or life periodically to recharge your batteries. A mental health day can do wonders for your happiness, creativity, and health.

Be sure to take the whole day to relax—don't fill it up with errands and appointments. Go for a long walk outside, enjoy a coffee at a local café, take a warm bath... Spend your time focusing on what your body needs to restore itself—you deserve it!

Visit a Lilac Garden

The unmistakable, fresh scent of lilacs in springtime is like a breath of fresh air after colder weather. When lilacs are in bloom where you live, go visit a lilac garden to savor the beauty of your flower. Search online for a lilac garden in your area—you might not have even realized it was there. On your visit, take deep breaths and walk slowly, treating it almost like a meditative experience. While you're there, take the opportunity to learn about the many varieties of lilacs, which can actually vary in color from white to deep purple.

Indulge in an All-Natural Body Scrub

Body scrubs can rejuvenate tired skin, wake up your senses, and calm your mind—plus, they feel amazing! An all-natural version is ideal for Virgo because it will connect you to the earth itself. Simply start with organic sugar or sea salt as a base, then add an appropriate carrier oil plus essential oils (diluting according to instructions) that match your needs or preferences. For example, try a lavender-vanilla scrub to complement a soothing bath. Or, wake up in the morning with the bright smells of a citrus blend. To use, gently rub a coating of the scrub to areas that need smoothing or exfoliation, then rinse off.

Try a Bentonite Clay Mask

B entonite clay is a natural volcanic ash found in Fort Benton, Wyoming. It contains minerals such as iron, magnesium, and potassium, and holds an electric charge that might draw toxins out of your skin when the clay is combined with water. The clay can also soften your skin, decrease the size of your pores, and even out your skin tone. To make a mask, use a plastic spoon to combine equal parts sodium bentonite clay (bought from a trusted source) with water or raw apple cider vinegar to make a paste in a nonmetal bowl (or follow the specific instructions on the packaging). Apply the mixture to your face and let it absorb and harden for 15–20 minutes, then rinse off and moisturize as normal.

Reach for Your Goals

Once earth signs know what they want, they will stay the course until they get it. Earth signs are strong and disciplined people, so use that tenacity to achieve the things you want most in life. Use your detail-oriented, driven brain and create a goal board. List the things you most want to accomplish and post them up where you can see them every day. This way you can be sure to keep your goals fresh in your mind and on the top of your to-do list. Also make sure the goals you write on your board are clear and actionable. Whatever your goal is, this visual reminder is key to helping you stay focused and on track.

Stretch Your Workout Routine

Earth signs enjoy having an established routine they can count on, so try developing a well-rounded workout routine that works for you. Add stretching as a consistent part of your routine to keep you feeling strong and healthy. Stretching can also prevent more serious injuries throughout your workout. Since stretching keeps your muscles flexible and relaxed, it's a perfect release if you're feeling stiff from a long day in the office, or even just tense and stressed. This easy, revitalizing addition to your workouts will make your body feel great.

Reduce Stress with Grounding

———————

I t's no surprise that earth signs should be in close contact with the earth itself. One way to literally connect with the earth is to try "grounding," or standing or walking barefoot outside on the grass, soil, or sand. Not only does being barefoot outside just feel good, it may also reduce stress and inflammation while improving your circulation and mood. Try to spend 30 minutes a day grounding—either all at once or broken up into smaller chunks of time. Afterward, you'll find yourself relaxed, restored, and recharged.

About the Author

Constance Stellas is an astrologer of Greek heritage with more than twenty-five years of experience. She primarily practices in New York City and counsels a variety of clients, including business CEOs, artists, and scholars. She has been interviewed by *The New York Times*, *Marie Claire*, and *Working Woman*, and has appeared on several New York TV morning shows, featuring regularly on Sirius XM and other national radio programs as well. Constance is the astrologer for *HuffPost* and a regular contributor to Thrive Global. She is also the author of several titles, including *The Astrology Gift Guide*, *Advanced Astrology for Life*, *The Everything® Sex Signs Book*, and the graphic novel series Tree of Keys, as well as coauthor of *The Hidden Power of Everyday Things*. Learn more about Constance at her website, ConstanceStellas.com, or on *Twitter* (@Stellastarguide).